LEVEL 3   EASY PIANO SOLO

Easy Hymn Solos
10 Stylish Arrangements by Wendy Stevens

ISBN 978-1-4234-7794-5

HAL•LEONARD®
CORPORATION
7777 W. BLUEMOUND RD. P.O. BOX 13819 MILWAUKEE, WI 53213

In Australia Contact:
Hal Leonard Australia Pty. Ltd
4 Lentara Court
Cheltenham, Victoria, 3192 Australia
Email: ausadmin@halleonard.com.au

Visit Hal Leonard Online at
www.halleonard.com

ALL CREATURES OF OUR GOD AND KING

Words by Francis of Assisi
Translated by William Henry Draper
Music from *Geistliche Kirchengesäng*
Arranged by Wendy Stevens

Majestically (♩ = 100)

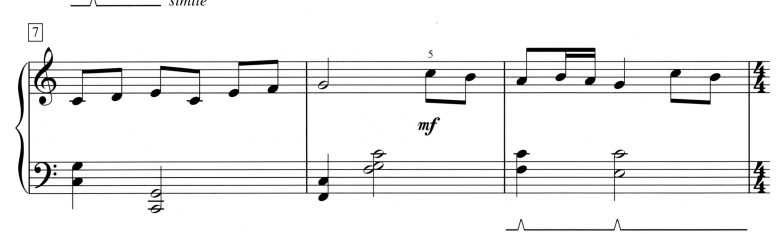

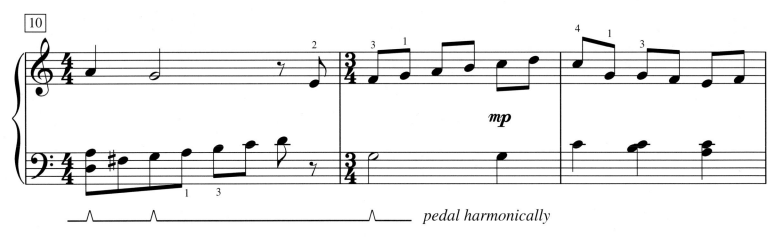

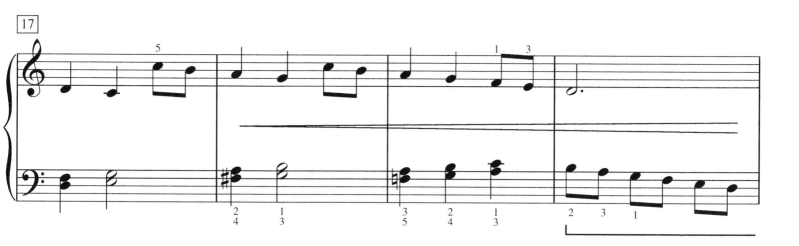

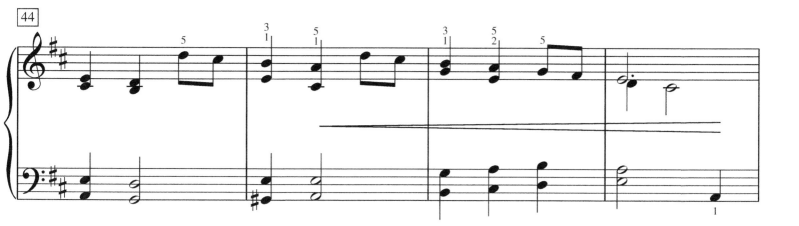

8vb

ALL THINGS BRIGHT AND BEAUTIFUL

Words by CECIL FRANCES ALEXANDER
17th Century English Melody
Arranged by Wendy Stevens

Peacefully (♩ = 104)

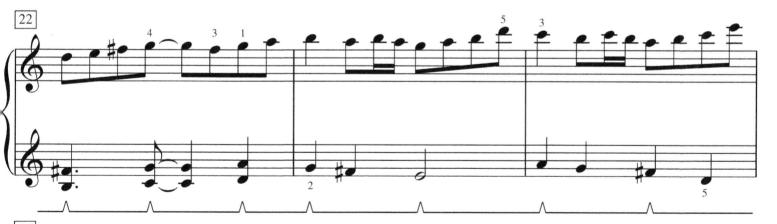

AMAZING GRACE

Words by JOHN NEWTON
Traditional American Melody
Arranged by Wendy Stevens

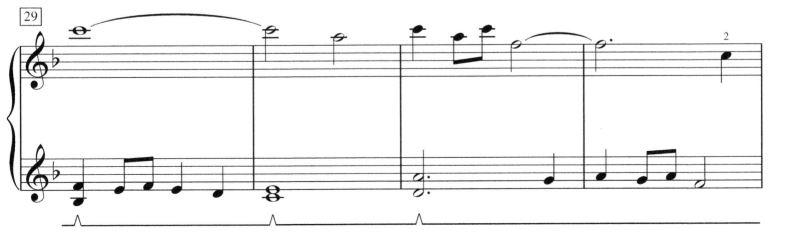

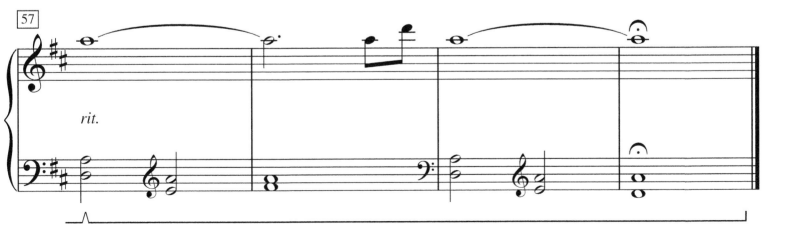

BATTLE HYMN OF THE REPUBLIC

Words by JULIA WARD HOWE
Music by WILLIAM STEFFE
Arranged by Wendy Stevens

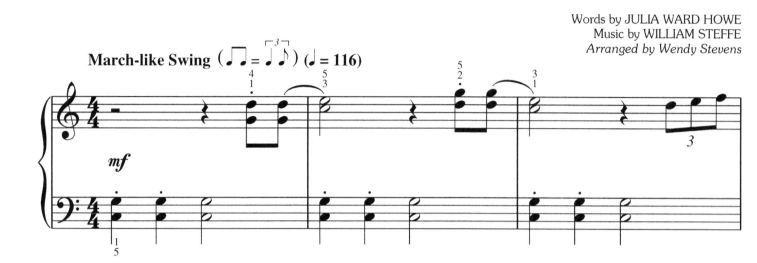

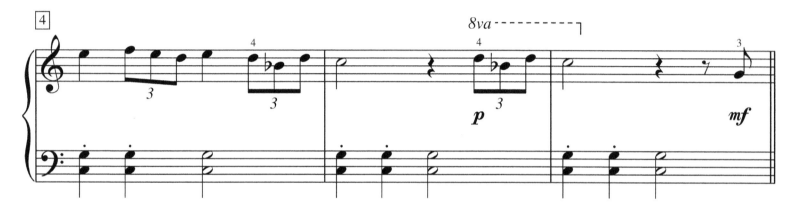

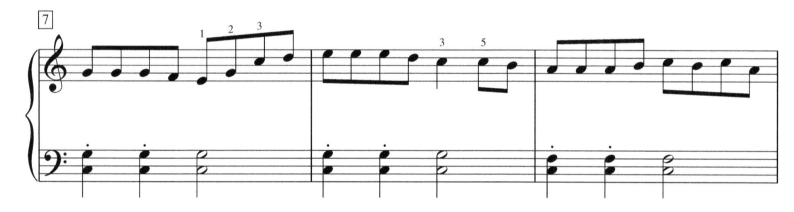

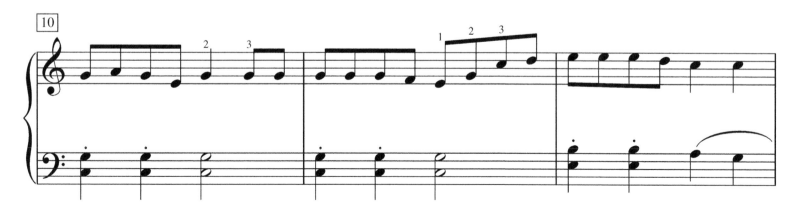

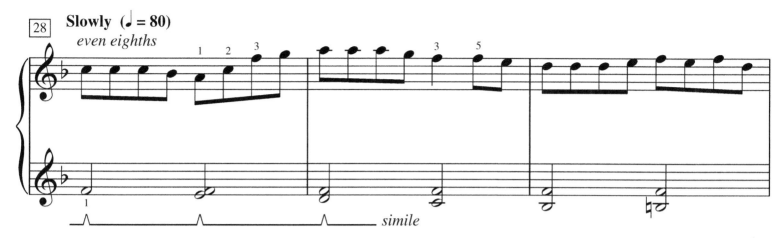

COME, THOU FOUNT
OF EVERY BLESSING

Words by ROBERT ROBINSON
Music from *The Sacred Harp*
Arranged by Wendy Stevens

Gently (♩ = 92)

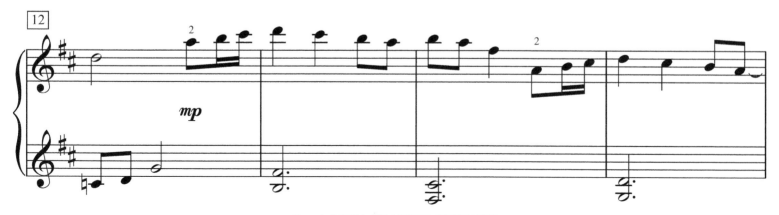

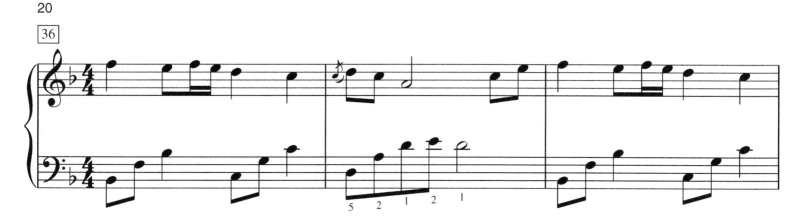

COUNT YOUR BLESSINGS

Words by JOHNSON OATMAN, JR.
Music by EDWIN O. EXCELL
Arranged by Wendy Stevens

Energetically (♩ = 120–132)

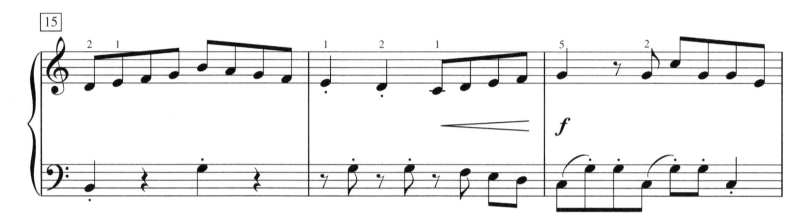

pedal harmonically

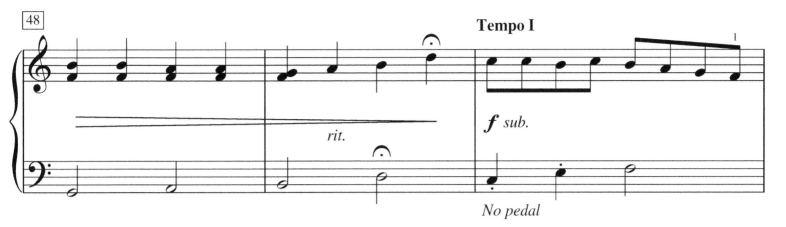

I SING THE MIGHTY POWER OF GOD

Words by ISAAC WATTS
Music from *Gesangbuch der Herzogl*
Arranged by Wendy Stevens

Joyfully (♩ = 126–138)

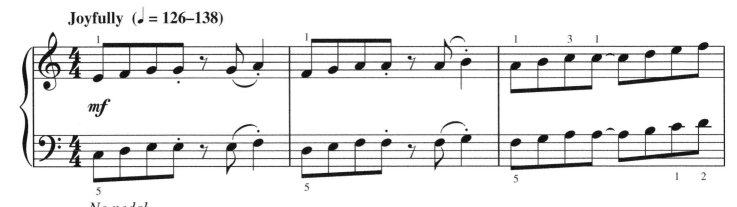

No pedal

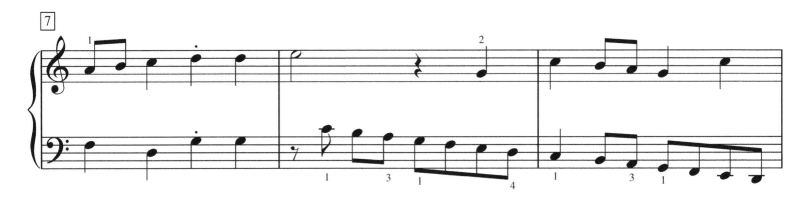

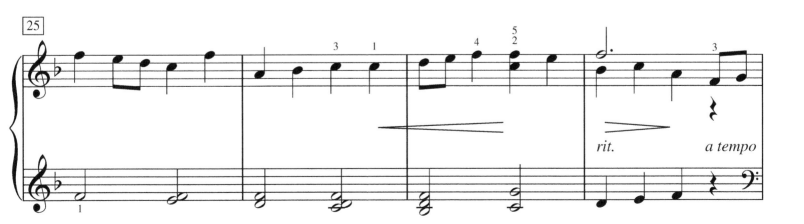

28

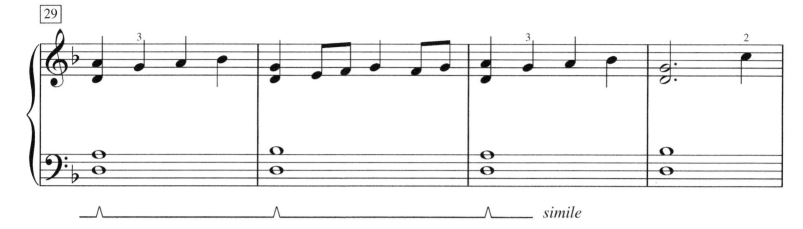

Slightly faster

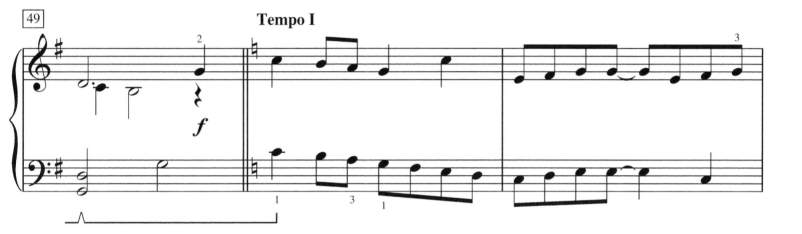

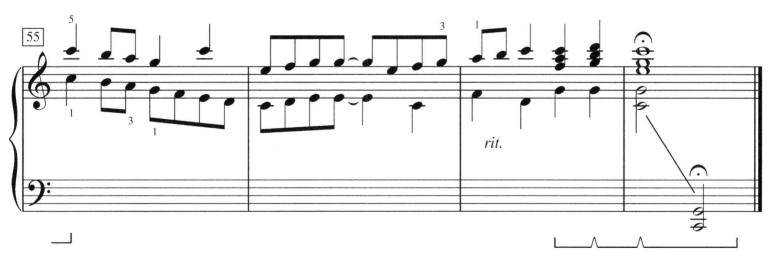

JESUS LOVES ME

Words by ANNA B. WARNER
Music by WILLIAM B. BRADBURY
Arranged by Wendy Stevens

Gracefully, distantly (♩ = 120)

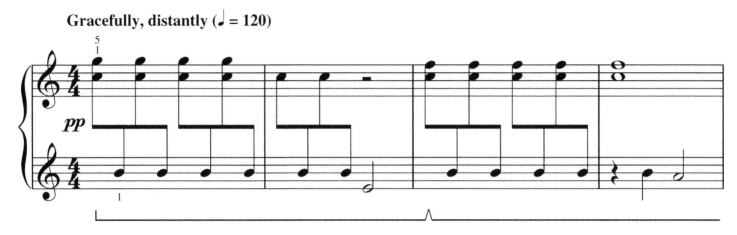

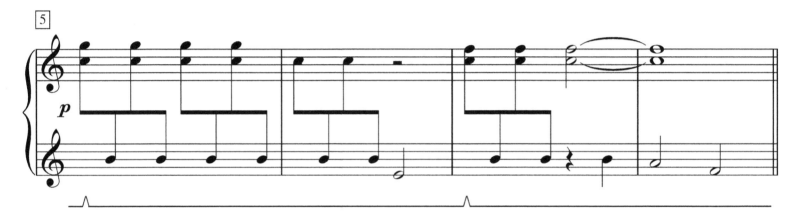

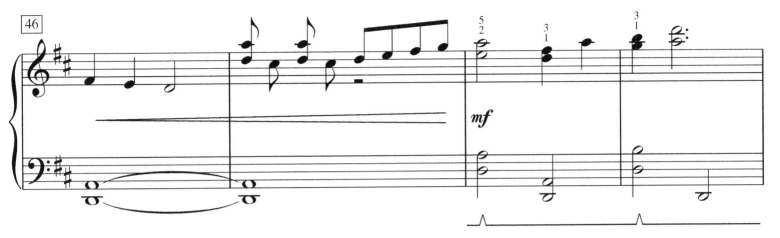

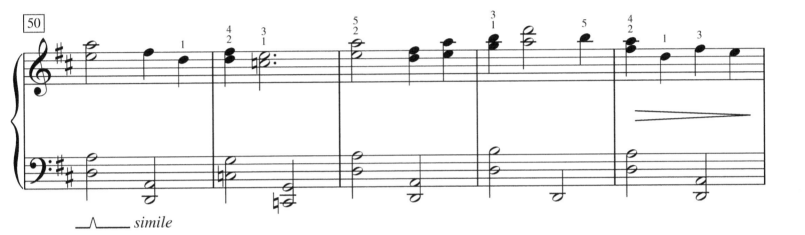

JOSHUA FIT THE BATTLE
OF JERICHO

African-American Spiritual
Arranged by Wendy Stevens

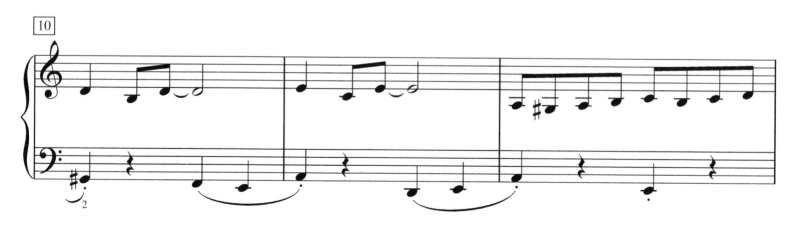

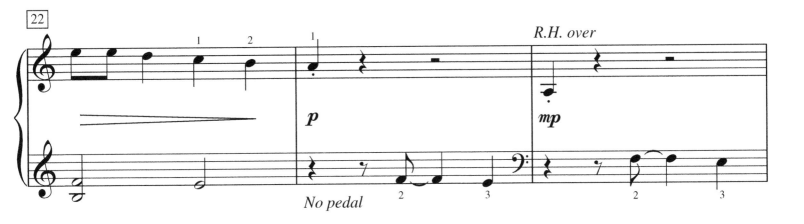

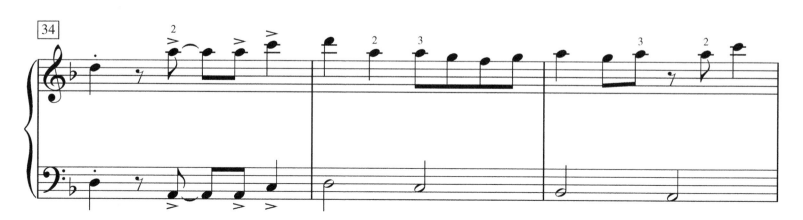

WADE IN THE WATER

Traditional Spiritual
Arranged by Wendy Stevens

With a groove (♩♩ = ♩♪) (♩ = 126–132)

No pedal

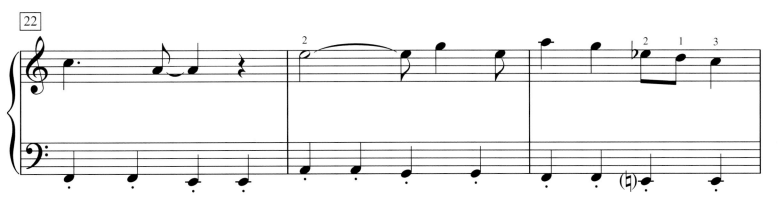

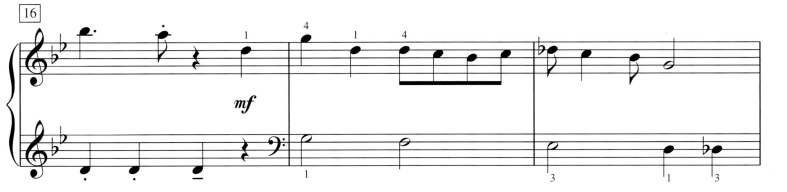

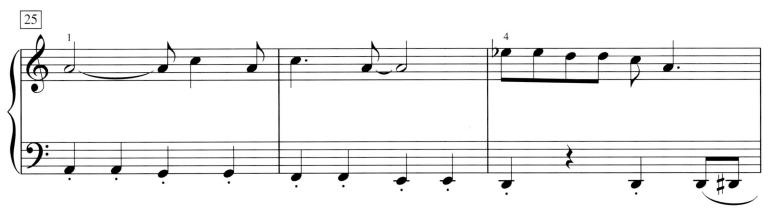

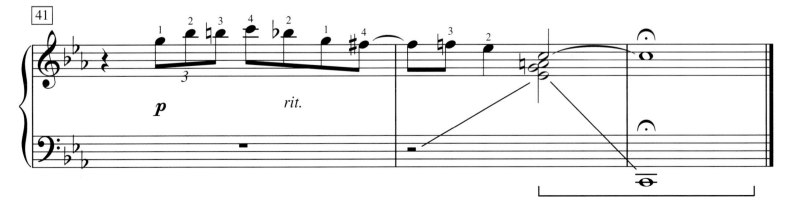